M000221147

SHE WHO DESTROYS THE LIGHT

A POETRY COLLECTION BY SHAHIDA ARABI

THOUGHT CATALOG BOOKS

Copyright © 2016 by Shahida Arabi

All rights reserved.

Published by Thought Catalog Books, a division of
The Thought & Expression Co., Williamsburg, Brooklyn.

For general information and submissions:

hello@thoughtcatalog.com.

Founded in 2010, Thought Catalog is a website and imprint dedicated to
your ideas and stories. We publish fiction and non-fiction from emerging and
established writers across all genres.

thought.is

Published by Chris Lavergne. Illustration by Fernanda Suarez. Art Direction &
Design by KJ Parish. Project Management by Alex Zulauf.

ISBN 978-1-945796-21-0

10 9 8 7 6 5 4 3 2 1

Printed in the USA

SHE WHO DESTROYS
THE LIGHT

Fairy Tales Gone Wrong

SHAHIDA ARABI

*Dedicated to the warriors who walk through fire,
yet continue to dream big dreams.*

You all deserve your happy endings.

THE HOLY TRINITY

CATHARSIS

RAPUNZEL

She is

Gentle, fiery

Weary from the battles

While you are the mad surgeon

Picking at her wounds

Nursing them no more

Turning and twisting her truth

To feed her falsehoods.

Trust her when she tells you—

That like Rapunzel she can spin

your hatred into gold.

Your put-downs into her power.

Your ugly words into her

incentive.

And your sabotage into her success.

You will soon learn

to never underestimate

a woman who has a

track record

of proving

her enemies wrong.

PRINCE CHARMING

I became accustomed to the cruelty and the raging storms

The silent glare followed by the teasing eyes

The sweet nothings and the callous words

Bruising the soul and battering the mind—

Carefully evaluating how far I could go.

I recoiled in

The hard grip of his hands

delicately tying my stomach into knots

Like a tailor making me a dress that would beautifully hug my thighs

And squeeze my throat at the same time.

I crawled into the chambers of my own heart and made a cage

Fenced myself in

Scribbled a message on the edges of the walls

Stop here and never again.

Only to sleep beneath the clouds at night

Wake up to the thunder and taste the rain

On his lips.

BLUEBEARD

He weaves his painful words into her skin like kryptonite
Always with a smirk and knowing eyes
A smug sadism knitted into the arch of his brow
His lips sewn into a scarecrow smile

THE MAN WITH TWO MASKS

I sold my heartbeats for a lived-in cage

A secondhand soul and a man I had never met

I met his doppelgänger

shook his hand and sought his lips

Merged his name with mine until I met the second man

Who I pretended did not exist.

He stole my kisses and my laughter, became a thief for my pride.

Year upon year went by,

Where one man would appear and the other disappeared,

One with a smile and the other with a glint in his eye.

My heart hung heavy and my mind deep-dived, headfirst

Cutting the cord between the two, pretending I never knew.

I reasoned that the second man was nothing like the first, though they looked the same—

swallowed my lies in tiny cups until they both

drowned me,

Annabel Lee in her tomb

by the sounding sea.

SANTA MONICA

Like art he sketches her
Burns vines into charcoals to paint her
In black ink across his blood
A tattoo of fire and life on his arm
She is the shadow resting on the lines of his palms
The creases in his cheeks
The gaze as he stares at the water
Looking into a mirror that never runs smooth
She is darkness brimming in his smiles
Sunset soaked in his silence
Choices tarnished by his voice
She is the pier on a busy street
where he has pounded all over the pavement
her ears reverberating
with the sound of his footsteps
his ugly words and his chokehold

PAPER DOLLS

Paper dolls and paper girls

Are like makeshift snowflakes

Each unique but to you they are the same

You touch their bodies as if they were papier-mâché

mold and maul them like clay

Pottery with a pretense

Punishment packaged in play

Each man rips pieces and keeps the fragments to himself

Calling it his art for the day

REMINDER

Do not let the world stifle your otherworldliness

Your gentle way of swaying to the wind

The rush of your feet on bare-naked floors

Dancing to the music as the record spins

Don't let the world take away your high-pitched laugh
and the freckles on your nose or the scars on your tongue

For speaking your truth so deeply the world became undone

SEVEN

Mishaps and misfits
they all shoulder their misfortunes here
A room filled with those they call
damaged
but all I see is a room
filled with broken wings
bearing puncture wounds
from dwarfed hearts.

INVISIBLE

One day the world will see you.

Do not believe the tall tales that

You deserved what you received unless

What you received was a long-standing agreement

That you were worthy, valuable.

It was not your fault that the world weaved messages

Into your skin and etched falsehoods into your brain

Telling you that you were nothing.

Even if your own mother silenced you

Even if your own father tore you apart

Even if charlatans warped the dimensions of your heart

Your soul is still made out of stardust

caked into the corners of your bones.

And divinity like that never lies.

And above all please remember that

Survivors

Should not be judged by those who have not

Lived their stories.

BEAUTY AND THE BEAST

The flash of his rage erupts like a swinging door

hitting her face punching her walls tearing her skin beating her senseless

Invisible she wraps her arms around herself like a child

berated broken belittled

black eyes are as good as black hearts

scraped knees as bad as warped words

Thick skin not enough for

the sticks and stones of his contempt

She never shows the wounds and the scars because they only exist within

In the dark holes of his own walls and the craters in her soul

HANSEL AND GRETEL

He left her crumbs for midnight

To follow his path when she went astray

He feasted on her starvation

Ate her anxiety for dinner

Cooked her until

she was a bundle of bones

and a tangle of nerves

trying to trace his voice

on the other end of the phone.

OZ

The man behind the curtain is as dark

as his first name

as empty and vacuous as the mask

resting on his face

as dead and calm as his eyes during crisis

the tongue limp in his mouth

ready to find the words

to twist and turn

every truth on the planet

magicians have the

courtesy to saw their ladies

in half

he splits his into a million pieces

ensuring they never learn

how to put themselves back together again.

FEAR

I heard it in

Your aching voice

The battle cry in your song

I felt your body quake

And your mind reawaken

Listening to every footstep, every breath.

Counting every shadow

Around the corner.

Avoiding the cracks on the sidewalks and the

Telltale mirrors reflecting photographs of the war.

Your heartbeat a trembling bird in a cage

Rattling its corners left to right

Wishing, hoping, praying, pleading, fighting

To be free.

But knowing your mistake was feeling like life was too short

Not to have scraped knees and a broken heart.

GLASS

I lay in the tomb of my own making

Spooning with the secrets I'd never told

Silence tasted golden on your lips and harsh to my ears

I stifled the truth and smiled through it all

A stranger on the cusp of madness

Whispered in my ear

as gentle as a butterfly wing

This isn't a grave

She said

It's a cocoon

It's not death it's life

Who knew rebirth could be more painful

More so than even

The last breath on the cross

SHAHIDA ARABI

LET DOWN YOUR HAIR

Your words like thin air

Floated above me as I struggled to pull

Them down to where they belonged

Pleading for gravity

The dirt awaited them but they crawled

Into my ears and into my head

Refused to leave and signed a new lease

Repeating themselves again and again

When cruel words were foreplay

Your touch like dry ice

Burned the roof of my mouth

So that I could no longer speak.

My voice shaken, I waited for your words to dissipate like rain only to have them cling to my skin

The droplets made a form-fitting dress

Pierced every inch of my body until I couldn't remember life before or life after or even life in between

Just your words with the half-life of an atom and the shelf life of a disease

Looking for a cure while you searched for a new host

THE ARTIST

There are haiku

written on the arch of your back

Poetry on your lips

Lengthy essays

lining your arms

words at the nook of your neck

short stories

bursting

from your hands

like the seams of an ill-fitted dress

LEAVE

Leave the man who uses your dreams

As doormats

wiping his feet as he comes and goes

Leave the man who sucks you dry so he can feel

What it is like to have a shadow of warmth inside of him

Your spirit pulsating like blood beneath his flesh

Telling you to have thicker skin

Leave the man who uses your body as shelter but not a home

Who uses his words as stones and his silence

 like sticks to bruise your broken bones

Leave the man who breaks your wings

And uses them as crutches

Just so he can learn to fly

FILM

I breathed in her beauty like a script
I wore it wrapped around my skin like newspaper
after a cold shower she clung to me like film.
I wrote her words and lived her life
until I remembered who I was

PAN

Tell me about the boy who never grows old
His face ages but his tantrums never end
Should we call him
A lost boy
or a malicious man?

CUTTHROAT

I like to see the sudden doubt

on his furrowed brow

As I use his weapons

as boomerangs

FILM NOIR

I wrote the stories and you played the script
A film noir where you were the darkness
I was light trying to find the switch
and squeeze through the few cracks
in the walls of a
windowless room
You were the night
devouring itself.

SHE WHO DESTROYS THE LIGHT[1]

I freeze

There is nothing keeping me warm

But the shivers that

Race through me.

Your wrath is like winter.

It leaves the taste of snow in my mouth.

December is the month of my birth.

Unfortunately, it is also the month

Of my death.

It was so easy for Venus to be reborn.

But me,

I scatter—

Like shards, each glass piece

reflecting

what I lacked

in the first place.

I can barely put them together

to make them

what they used to be.

And you, you

1   This is the meaning of the name "Persephone."

leave the shards in

perfect disorder.

And you, you don't make it any easier

And you, you are as cruel as Hades

because when I shiver and clatter my teeth,

you block the sun, and your shadow

is as large as the canvas I am trying to paint on.

Even the sparrows[2] know you're coming.

I can hear their silent screams, as if crows

Are swooping

down upon their feast.

You take me down to the underworld,

where there is no springtime,

and, like Persephone,

I am the prisoner of your will.

Your touch is a dead harvest.

Your words sink like pomegranate seeds

into my ears, each

a drop

too

soon.

---

2   Sparrows were Aphrodite's signs.

THE EDIBLE WOMAN

little red riding hood force-feeds him a spoon

what the wolf devours—

he devours in doom

a quiet climate

but a deafening clamor

these were the things she whispered in his ear

she stared into his monstrous eyes, awakened for the first time and said

here is a little dinner for today

dine and dash, I am done being the prey

consume me like an edible woman

but I feast on wolves as they howl at the full moon

beneath my red armor I am my own savior

I consume the consumer, I eat my predator's words

I mold them and shape them into bright clay

I blow out the candles to breathe in the dark

I am not the little girl who cried wolf

but rather I tear the sheep's clothing to reveal the vices within

I snuggle up closer to the criminal to test its cage

once the bars open there is a performance to be staged

crooning at the moon he thinks the play is done

but I devour him with my fangs, bury him with my red cape

where there were two wolves

now there is only one

MEMORY

Some memories are erased

Some are airborne

And some are cast in stone

Etched like a carving

While others are evasive like

A red scarf in the wind unraveling

Pieces, fragments, red flags—

Fractured like kites

 slinking into the night.

FUGUE

Like slivers of your former self

You came masquerading

hiding your essence until the moment you needed

A new mask.

Never fear the offender who breaks open the skulls of his
friends so openly

Fear the friend who sneaks up behind to thrust your head
to the guillotine

under the pretense of a kiss

Fear romance with the hint of premeditated murder

Fear the occasional cruelty with sweeping kindness

Grand gestures with closeted small-mindedness

Fear the man or woman who charms their guests

And enslaves their spouse

Fear the crocodile tears

hiding the dark hearts of monsters in your bed

IMPACT CRATERS.

There were many inside her;
she was as bumpy and convoluted
as the paths on the moon.
the
curvature of her throat
and a bashful smile; these are her most
beautiful defects—
could he be the earth, shining because of her?
The black holes in her baggage begged to differ—
no one could carry them so soon
So she buried them on her back and went on her way
Tiptoeing across each crooked trapdoor
Until she fell like Alice to her doom.

BLACK

The maiden took her first bite of the fruit

As he slithered down her back the snake hissed in her ear

It was all meant to be my dear

Soul mates arrive when no one is watching

They clutch your heart and then wrap around your throat

LITTLE RED

The woman with the red coat and long legs
Even longer hair sits cross-legged breathing
Her mantras a litany of
Blessings trapped in the tones of
Fuck you
Her eyes an outpouring of words she can never say
Her body a warrior stance in limbo of a child's pose
Her meditation a lisp of rage
Seething through her teeth
Crackling fire in her bones
I stared at her and locked eyes
She is tenderness wrapped in depravity
A quick wit locked by the bars of propriety
She blinked and smiled forcefully
Exhaled
Disappeared into herself
Never to be seen again

MALIBU

I'll drive you to the water at sunset

Watch the sun beat on the scars of your hands

Feel your pulse beneath the sand

Making castles out of lightning bolts

scribbling tiny miracles and synchronicities on your arm

Sleep in the nook of your neck until dusk

And kiss you goodbye at dawn

Make a bed for you in the water

Watching you sink and sail away like a ship

SACRILEGE

What if miracles had little to do with
The scripture written in your books
and everything
to do with God in your laughter?

CRUCIFIXION

THE ARCHIVES

The crucifix
of your sentences
dig into
me,
and my heartbeat
pounds, scared to death
of the axe that you grind.
Torn from the pages
of a mind
regurgitating full cycle
your words
fly like paper airplanes
first brushing against my ears
but then
like sharpened knives
twisting and turning
my brain does a pirouette and inside my mind
all the paper cuts bleed.

LURED

He drinks until he sleeps

Still awake he calls her with

his eyes like a white shark

Feeds on

The blank space of his rage and the slump of her defeat

His words like bullets

Shooting blanks into her system, pumping her with

The trickles of doubt, his comfort her heroin

Her despair, the blood that trickles down his chin

NARCISSUS AND ECHO

Dorian Gray

sits on my sidewalk

looks up at me with his charming grin

and his nauseatingly good looks

His youth like parchment on his skin

his lies sugarcoated, rose-colored glasses

as gray as the old painting he trades for the truth,

ready to take my world for another spin.

O.C.D.

The girl with no name showers
in the dark, long threads of hair
climbing her head, she cleanses
until the faucet of words seep
through her brain
unplugged, all the thoughts in excess
pour down the drain.
Gnawing, the point edge of thought
creeps in like the cadaver of forgotten memory,
a corpse revived again, sinks its
teeth into skin and tears into flesh,
stuck, there is no going back
just the same

record playing again.

this thought

breeds,

eats itself alive, vomits, then again swallows itself whole like

a serpent curling

bending in a circle

feeding itself new life,

new death.

She cuts the noose, but he's in her head,

the thought that lives all of its nine lives;

leaps upon its feet, murders, and

multiplies.

GASLIGHTING

He spins gravity and twists and turns
Her words until her world is tipped over
Plunging over the edge of its own axis
In his realm light is dark and peace is chaos
He creates a dark room for her which she now calls shelter
Comforted in the arms of her murderer

REBIRTH

If other worlds are possible

Then the reality you live in right now can change any instant in any moment

Perhaps in an earth-shattering sentence

The sudden end of a long drought

or the slow movements of a season

Slowly but surely turning.

Underworlds can become gardens

Growth can sprout from

death and dreams planted from the same seed

And the scars on your wrists can be rewritten by new words.

HAUNTED

All my ghosts were haunted by their own ghosts
All my coffins filled by the thirst in your bite
You wanted more once you learned I had more
A lifetime's supply of lifeblood
Corpses posing as soul mates.

EVER AFTER

A father that does not love his daughter

sets her up for a life of pain

the heartache with no name lasts forever because it is never a heartache

it is just a dull perpetual empty ache

a void where fairy tales always end and monsters begin

THE WOLF

She says no and he yanks the dress over her head

I watch from afar

float from the ceiling not knowing whether I am alive or dead he censors her pleas and crouches at her knees ripping her wide open until she says *please*

Stop.

sick to my stomach I am a wisp of a ghost the red dress by her side as she finally goes silent

Listening to his phone call late at night

watches as he disposes of her

drives her

to another home and the next morning she cannot stay awake and saves the red dress in a black bag

spends hours at the hospital slowly swallowing the pills they give her until each one turns her world pitch-black

her fever reaches a high point and her blood literally boils

she is naked for the world to see

to inspect

they climb into the very sacred spaces where he tried to claim her

Trying desperately to find the wounds he had left.

SHAHIDA ARABI

LOVE-BOMBING

Her love is his meditation

A mirror for the self-absorbed

A break from his shame

His love is her reflection

Of herself.

A dual mirror

Showcasing

The parts of herself

She has always hidden

She finds them suddenly adored, cherished, filled with grace.

Until one side of the mirror

Splits open

An earthquake that erupts

And cracks into pieces on the other side

Of the world they have co-created

Now in fragments

They must put together

Alone.

MARY MAGDALENE

Death becomes her
and life defends her
As God holds her hair back,
she heaves
into the dark corners of the streets,
missing each piece of herself.
A holiness still remains
in the dark underworld of her
Thoughts, each draped with the promise
Of a second coming.

KARMA

I collected your silence in my cup and drank

Sipped quietly until

all

the

words

settled, burning holes into my skin.

I kept your secrets buried beneath my tongue

Your transgressions

behind closed doors,

Until one day in public view

You pulled out the words, plucked them from my flesh like needles

Raised the hairs on the back of my neck

Each year after was a different city, a different name—

And for the first time in a long time,

I relished the silence when you were gone

HANSEL

I see the mother reprimand her son who grimaces, looks up at me in sudden shame before his eyes quickly flicker away like a flame that has been put out on the palm of someone's hand

and the way his shoulders melt like wax when they slump tells me how much

it burns

THE GRAVE

I have burned the fat photos

Like I have burned my flesh

I have rattled my skin against my bone

Cradled my death

Held flabby skin in my hands

Until all the fat dragged to my knees until all of them said

Yes please,

They say, "Oh my, you've lost weight."

"I was just going to say you look so thin—"

And before I was what?

And before I was what?

Answer this. "I was close to dying, this is why I am thin—"

"Oh, but you look so good. Good job."

"I was writing my will while I was this thin—"

"Everyone likes losing weight."

"I was crawling in my grave to eat the dirt I was so thin—"

"The grave suits you."

Oh yes.

The grave suits me,

Fits like second skin.

SCARLET

The room hung heavy with subtle digs
The shadowed glances and telltale whispers
Of people who knew nothing about anything at all.

ICE

She is brittle to the touch and fragile to the bone yet the strongest in her light. I see the way she hides her bruised arms and callused palms her scarred neck and her black eyes her head lowered and a tender smile that doesn't quite belong. She is the Red Sea, missing in action as she is parted, broken and miraculous. I see the way she walks with her shoulders slumped and her feet hesitant to step on the cracks on the sidewalk. One day when someone sees her I will see her eyes brighten with recognition and her back straighten with pride. Perhaps the crease in her smile will become a grin and joy will mark her laughter again. One day when she is curled up in the sheets of a safe haven maybe in the arms of someone truly safe she will feel it is okay to finally sleep again without both eyes open

scared of the dark and the darkness in men

LETTER FROM AN EMPATH TO A TOXIC PERSON

While I love to be the healing balm

To another person's ache

I am not responsible for fixing your life

or catering to your toxicity.

I am not responsible for managing your triggers,

walking perpetually on eggshells

or telling you what you want to hear

in order to keep the peace.

I am not the war zone where you can drop your bodies

The closet where you can hide your many skeletons.

I hold the key to the home that is my life

and you can no longer unlock me.

I am not your standby relief from the shame you need
to heal.

I do not own your wound and I refuse to let your wound

Own me.

I am not your emotional punching bag nor am I your emotional sponge.

I do not exist for your pleasure or as a site for your projected pain.

My responsibility is to myself—to be my own person and stay true to myself—

to heal my own wounds

my own triggers and terrors—

Giving, authentically, to those who give to me

without depleting myself in the process.

THE VORTEX

They swallow her whole
Spit and chew the pieces that don't fit in
With the mold
They create a sculpture
Of light and dark
Paint her a portrait of
What the world should see
Black and white
Grays for the frame
But when she paints herself
There are colors and cracks and scratches
Brokenness wrapped in
the blankets of war and peace.

BLACKOUT

The disease in his mind is the

Disease in her soul

Eating her alive each time

He takes a

sip too many

GASLIT

He tells her to medicate her feelings

Seek a therapist for daring to see the truth

He paints the edges dark and calls them white,

Misplaces all notions of wrong and right

Denies the shadows on the walls and the lipstick on his collar

And the smell of her perfume

SHAHIDA ARABI

DUSK

She was sheltered by the droplets

Cascading that fall morning

The first day of September she remembered

Wrapping her arms around herself and smiling

For the first time in a long time there was hope at the corners of her cheeks

Dawn where there was usually dusk.

WRITER

She lived the life of a writer, fed too many stories

Hungry for more words—

starving senseless

she dreamed of rewriting

Editing these scars

Cleaning the dust off

Old secrets and scattered books

The ones about star-crossed lovers

Filling her room with glass slippers

No feet have ever fit into.

Translating her battle wounds into your verses

And her pain into your poetry.

THE EVIL STEPMOTHER

The girl smokes outside the bar until

all the flames in her head ignite

she breathes in and out as

legs are moving past and words are pouring out from
the side of

her clenched jaw.

He comes out, his eyes, once playful, now imploring—

Mother and daughter are now at war again—

a war his wife never asked for, a war she never sought to fight.

Fists are clenched and the door is closing

It is time for mother to weed out his "bad habit"

and to excel at her own.

The girl with the cigarette will be put out

the stump of her body and her spirit like a wet cigar

crushed by her three-inch heel and her shrill voice.

It's important to remember that

some wolves wear dresses and a fur coat—

Some thrones are gently taken

while others are destroyed.

SHIFT

There's nothing like

blood-curdling disappointment

roaring at the pit of your stomach

sinking in your throat

each expectation lowered as you climbed higher

Knowing it was

Never enough

Nothing like the tiny betrayals

Replaying themselves over and over again

Like a maze in the brain that loops for a lifetime

MIRACLES

Tiny miracles are often born out of
shaky missteps and
nervous
laughter.
The synchronicity of
destiny disguised as
accidents, of growth masquerading
as pain.

NIGHTMARES

I touched her hand underwater and we stared at each other across oceans

Fingers touching fingers, palms resting upon palms

Mirror, mirror on the wall

who is the most broken of them all?

The lost child or the lost woman?

The girl who always aches or the woman who never sleeps?

As she bowed her head I cradled her in my arms

The mother she never had

Watching as she closed her eyes

And sang her the last lullaby.

DETOX

Each dose came with a price

A mouthful of pain and pleasure

Withdrawal was depletion, erasure

Erosion of the safe haven that

Kept me in danger.

HISTORY

She cradled her head with her palms
A lost child silencing the screams of her
Mother and father
Her ears shut out the rage
Her eyes her first portrait of the contempt
That seemed to follow her for years to come.
Her voice stifled, echoing in the chambers of her chest
Her bed sheets and blankets a refuge
Years go by
And her heart becomes gold and steel
Hardened by the hardship and softened by
The willingness to give all that she did not receive
And never saw anyone else in her life receive.
She grew up to give the love that she never felt
She grew up to wipe the tears of others
And hold their hands when they were alone

She knows what it is like to lie awake

Five days straight without seeing sunlight

Creating another fortress of bed sheets and pillows

To keep her warm

Saying her prayers quietly so as not to make a sound

She knows what it is like to wake up and know that

Out of all the love she gave, some of which she'd
never receive,

The real love story was the people she reached

In their dark hours of midnight, reaching for their third
bottle of

Wine or pills or the poison of their choice.

The orphans of the childless parents who never knew

How to honor their own children.

To touch the heart of another lost child,

That was the realest love she'd ever felt.

HIGH

I raised
the roof
with my expectations again
Basic decency and respect.

THE MAD HATTER

We place the boys and girls in cages

Medicate their rage and wrap them in the white sheets of hospital beds

Hide them in windowless rooms, asking them to paint what they rarely see

We close their eyes and ask them to keep quiet about their anxiety

To tiptoe through their sadness and stifle their weeping as they sleep

We warn them not to harm themselves, while placing them in the very places they are harmed: loud voices and shrieking screams, smirking doctors and unruly patients, the knowledge of their separateness.

Feeding them placebos we call medicine,

We never ask which ones are criminals and which ones

Were the victims of silent crimes, crimes that can't be spoken

Crimes for which healing can't be prescribed

READ THIS DURING THE
WORST MOMENTS OF YOUR LIFE

Read this when your heart is aching and your spirit is broken, when you're on your knees, depleted and defeated. Read this when you want to give up but there's a tiny part of you that still whispers *hold on for dear life*; read this when your faith has been shaken and your life has been split into fragments you can't seem to put back together. Read this when each day feels like a black hole, dragging in, distorting and destroying every sliver of light you once had.

Read this and take a deep breath, because yes, this is so painful and yes it seems hopeless, but no, it rarely is. Sometimes, panic is a reminder that we still want to hope for the things we've lost hope for, and tragedy is a reminder that we can still feel in a world that doesn't want us to. Sometimes, when we feel like we're sleeping our way through life, we're really reawakening to the truth. It's never easy taking the red pill or casting light on the shadows of the cave you once mistook reality for, but sometimes it's a necessary evil we swallow, because each trapdoor could be the portal to the path that leads us anywhere but here.

The truth is, grieving is never a straight line, it comes full circle and we might be forced to live through it again and again. Healing is never linear; it's a maze of distortions, confusion, smoke and mirrors, pain that was never spoken and invisible scars, battle wounds that never made it to the surface. The worst wars may be fought alone and inside your own head. Recovery has no timeline, no deadline, and no concrete measure like pills in a cup—in fact, forcing yourself to heal or comparing your healing to others is a prescription of poison rather than a cure. The best way to heal is to know that there are some things that cannot be healed, won't be healed or aren't meant to be healed in the ways we think they are—they're meant to be channeled and transformed.

The truth is, what feels like your crucifixion doesn't have any quick fixes. Time or words alone can't always soothe the wounds that can't be put into language. Trauma can speak in a foreign tongue and weave its code into every cell—this is the type of pain where the body and the mind both keep the score. Sometimes the only Band-Aids you have are platitudes mixed with raw truth—the days where you feel like you won't survive and the days where you learn you can, and all the moments in between.

The shock of the pain may never fully go away, it's just numbed and buried beneath tombs, beneath new memories, waiting to erupt through the cracks and crevices left open in your thoughts. Thoughts that wrap around your body like a chokehold, never seeming to let go. But in these thoughts, there are gaps, opportunities to interrupt the old tapes playing in the background, frozen in time.

That's because experiencing overwhelming pain doesn't mean you shouldn't try to sketch new thoughts or paint new memories, because pain can be as transformative as the art on a torn canvas. It can make you appreciate all the small joys you'd never think to relish. You are forced to remember the things you took for granted, the ones that appeared minuscule, and realize their larger-than-life roles in the grand scheme of things. In truth, pain is the excuse you needed to embrace all you have to be grateful for and all the things you fear losing so much you'll now work even harder to keep.

Because when you feel like you're dying, pain reminds you to savor the things that matter, the things worth fighting for.

The worst moments in your life can be both enlightening and severely unfair. They can be a melting pot of breakthroughs and breakdowns, the epicenter of your epiphanies and the core cause of your hopelessness; they can drown you or they can be the push you really need, so long as you remember to come up for air.

And it's always somewhat morbid to remember that the worst moments of your life *now* won't be the same ones in the future—but then again, neither will the best moments of your life—those are still yet to come, too. What you define as the worst and the best will change and ironically, the knowledge that there is an even worse hell ahead can provide some heavenly relief. Because if there's still worse pain than the one you feel now, you know you can survive this to experience the best version of joy.

When you breathe through what you've been through and remember all the days that you survived and all the days you didn't want to, you'll remember the brief moments that were so important, the quick snapshots of your life that delayed you burying your head in the sand, never to come out again. The ones that made you use the voice you silenced—the voice trapped within for years. The strange happenings that made you smile for the first time in weeks, the rare kindness of strangers who lent a hand, or the surprising reminders that God still laughs even when you've forgotten how.

Don't worry if you're no longer running toward your destination or if you're on your way to a free fall into the unknown. Don't worry if you aren't where you need to be, or if there are circumstances beyond your control that make you feel out of control. Don't worry even if you are at the height of everything you've ever wanted and you're afraid to look down to see how far you'd fall if you lost your footing.

Don't lose hope if your worst nightmares came true in the past or if someone tries to crush your dreams into a pulp in the present—because big dreams can never be destroyed by the small-minded people that were never brave enough to live out their own.

Don't worry if one day the pain seems to be at a standstill and you forget the old narratives running through your head, or if you rewrite your story even before you've lived another tale. Don't be afraid of your own powerlessness, and don't be afraid of your own power.

In the worst moments of your life, it's helpful to remember that when a chrysalis appears to shake violently, it's actually not breaking, it's warding off predators— and that sometimes when it turns black, it's actually unfolding into something new. Destruction can be the incentive for creation and self-protection. Crucifixion, the pathway for resurrection.

The pause in between, a much-needed hibernation that happens before rising once more.

Yet change isn't always so immediate, or easy or even gratifying or desirable. Sometimes, change is a slow spin of the world on its axis and gravity is the only thing keeping you grounded. Even the most glorious changes are excessively painful during the time we go through them. We don't look back at those deaths the same way we do when we're in the midst of dying—we don't see them as rebirths, we see them as cruel fates we don't deserve.

But rest assured that one day in the future there will be the privilege of more awakenings and of more happiness than you can capture in photographs; new growing pains and new first drafts. Rest assured that if you do not give up now, you'll get to change the course of everything that's still unwritten.

By the same token, we learn the hard way that tiny miracles can begin in shaky missteps—the first time we learn how to walk instead of crawl.

WARRIORS

I dance with the souls that know no one

That have never felt the safety of shelter

Or the haven from the storm

That have their skeletons buried

Far away from shore

I meet with the forgotten

Hand in hand

Prayer to prayer

Wound to wound

Go with them to battle

Or what's left of their silent war

REVOLUTION

Sometimes a girl's quietest revolution
Is loving her imperfect body and heart
Without any explanations
Or apologies

THE HUNTRESS

If you meet a man whose words chill your soul and take

Your mind for a spin,

You've met a man who will always feel like he's lost

When you win.

Tall,

dark

and cruel

Fluent in mismatched words and actions.

One hourglass needed

to measure his momentary conscience.

No other woman could defeat him

Until he meets his equal

The woman who will use his evil for her fuel.

Eats his cruelty for breakfast with a spoon

And hunts down hunters for her next meal

Whispers to the wolf,

I am the wolf and I am the hunter of wolves.

STARDUST

You are dark matter

Distorting my light

Convincing me that my galaxies

Are made of mere fog

Rather than the stardust

shining through my skin

shattering you into space.

WORTHWHILE

She merges with the stranger on the street

The rare kindness

and the warmth of his smile

a tenderness that is foreign

TRAVIS

To write poetry you need to get on your knees

Crawl into the deepest darkness of your widowed soul

Marry your pain to the page and paper.

Divorce your ego.

Wait for your brain to jumpstart the engine of your cookie-cutter lines

Inhale the verses you could never speak

And exhale what you allow everyone to see.

You need to know when to stop speaking and when to start,

Where to create the chapters without butchering the art

Of wearing your heart on your sleeve

So

You can take your cotton candy

feel-good poetry

and sugarcoat your verses

until they taste like honey at your lips

while I take my unbreakable truth

weave it around myself like a

stone-cold corset

wrap myself up in the reality

of regret of struggle of strife

You can take the death of

your creative faculties

while I choose the honesty of life.

Breathing and reviving

old dust into new words

While you make a house

for your falsehoods

and your saccharine

sweetness.

BULLY

the sharp words they plunged

like tiny fangs inside me

converting fire into ice and ice into flames

once dead upon my feet I revised myself

rewrote the narrative and came alive again

so you can spend your days doubting and plotting

to destroy me

but I will take your kingdom for a spin

with your hatred I will build my empire

with your spite I will access my crown

with your biting remarks I will turn

my coals into diamonds

transform my crisis into catharsis

my crucifixion

to my resurrection

COMPASSION

I tried to imagine you as a caged animal
Trapped and helpless
Small and alone
But it did nothing to ease the disgust and the shame
Of knowing that anyone could quietly murder
The soul of someone they claim to love
with such pride.

EVOLUTION

When society learns that
the length of a girl's skirt
is not a measure
of her consent—
we will see a revolution.
When daughters are taught how to heal
themselves more often than they are taught
how to become as thin as paper
we will see a revolution
When sons are taught how to tap
into the power of allowing themselves
to be whomever they wish to be
rather than masking their sensitivity with violence
we will see a revolution
when daughters and sons are touched with
love and gentleness rather than bearing witness
to war zones at home
we will see evolution.

HEARTSTRINGS

Lawless in the way they take things,
Thieves of the soul murder
Every source of joy
Butchering anything that drives your pulse
Or makes you weak at the knees
They sever it—
The very things they can sense
serves a reason for your heartbeat

TERRITORY

Words stamped like tattoos on the brain
Are white noise bleeding on the pages of the mind
Never ceasing to run through the same story again.
Buried beneath the bare bones of
Vague memories, she wears her sharp pain like skin,
Wraps it around her body
like a winter coat.

TURNING POINT

You broke the pattern
Interrupted the storyline
The narrative every girl writes for herself
The rules bent and the ice shed
Melted from my bones and into your lips

MAGIC

Tell me what it takes for the king to fall
For the queen to falter and the prince to relinquish it all
Tell me what it takes to take the throne
From those who clean the blood off the bones
of the people they have disposed of

WAKE-UP CALL

Each dream is a short awakening

A brief glance into who we are meant to be

Do not quietly store your dreams into the desk drawers
of someone else's playbook and expect to play large when
you have set out to spend your days filling in the numbers
of nothing more than a timesheet, a measure of the hours
you used to

build someone else's vision

when you could've been falling in love with your own.

CRIMINAL

One day when karma's footfall interrupts
Your daily grind
As they do all old men and women
who lived with many but have died alone,
I hope you remember her name
on the tip of your tongue
the men and the women you murdered
without a trace.

　　　　　　　　　　　　SHAHIDA ARABI

ALONE

She spends her days in laughter

dances until she is no longer afraid

Sips coffee in her bubble baths

Plays the music no one else will ever hear.

She relishes the moments where no one is breathing heavy

Dragon fire on the back of her neck

with the stench of alcohol on his breath.

She travels alone to faraway lands

Cultivates the very dreams and visions

He tried to pull from the root and eradicate

Awakes by herself to the dawn, enjoying the solitude.

CREDIT CHECK

Portraits of your family as you cut through them with glee

Treasuring your treasure chest

The trust fund baby

Cradles the numbers accounts for every cent unaccounted for

Lures his partners into the debt they never asked to incur

Have me invest more so you can cut back on your own investment

Rip the rug from underneath me

Pretend I was always in poverty

When in truth I was rich in honesty

And you were stingy with your lies

You were always the broke one living on the heart of another

I was just broken

　　　　　　　　　　　　　　　　　SHAHIDA ARABI

STEPSISTER

Push me over the edge

To the pinnacle of your hate

And there I'll make a bed and learn to create

Kingdoms out of your thorns

Music out of your makeshift tales

Books out of your cruelty

Poetry out of your crimes

Art out of your wounds

rub the salt on my scars

To prepare my scarlet letters

as victories

SHATTER

Switchblades and crusades
their words cut deep creating false
Memories and imaginary figments
Of self,
the woman wakes up not knowing where time went
or space fled
A rupture in her glassy eyes
A blankness in her smile she steps forward
Seeing a different her in the mirror

　　　SHAHIDA ARABI

RESURRECTION

THE GIRL WHO WALKS ON FIRE

The girl who has walked barefoot on flames

Knows that the truth could kill her.

Yet the slump of her shoulders

Can't compete with

The arch of her back and

the ashes beneath her feet.

This is a girl who can turn water into fire

And fire into rebirth.

This is the girl who can taste death

A thousand times

And use it to relish life.

The tomb that has been built for her

Is the only throne she's ever left,

time and time again

To rise again.

So they may try to dig a new grave

But know, you can never destroy a girl

Whose will is stronger than your ego

and bigger than your name.

SHAHIDA ARABI

THE GLASS COFFIN

Her mind creates maps of the unknown

Delights in the strange

She dances with her eyes, sighs with her feet

and smiles with her pain

until they bury her light

in their laughter

FULL

Once upon a red moon

The wolf now hid from the girl

Who walked across the forest with her feet planted firmly
on the ground

buried like tree trunks

Her head raised high and her certainty

More dangerous than his hunger

MIDNIGHT

when you hit her
you brought out the lioness
the one who ate your head
the head of a criminal
worthy of a guillotine
make no mistake—
she will never be defeated now
she raised her hand against you
pushed you with equal force
rewrote history
in the palm of her hand
victory
did you know—
now abusers must pay
by
the rules of physics
every action
will have an
opposite
reaction

the woman on the floor will rise up

the tight hand on the wrist will be shaken

the victim will be made victor

and the world will be ruled by

little girls with hearts

made out of gunpowder and lead.

SNOW WHITE

I gave you the luxury of my word
you gave me the poverty of your promises
the single-handed backhanded slap you felt was overdue
I turned around and you were through
pretending. I heard your voices and they were clear
I was the scapegoat and she was crowned the queen
falsely wrapped in your esteem
a dream you had fabricated years ago
so keep on pretending she steals the show
but I refuse to be the woman behind the curtain
the one who builds the kingdoms and forges paths
only to have them destroyed by her hand
She may have fooled you with her false mask
but I will rip it open for all to see.
Once, she left me for dead
but felt the panic when she saw me breathe
Realized—
I don't die out that easily.
I come alive again and ignite everything into flames
The girl who was once invisible
Now everyone shall know her name.

THE UNIVERSE

We pondered the view, the universe. The view was the universe

the city lights stretched out for miles with the ocean beside it

Birthdays and miracles. We stretched ourselves out like candle wax

my feet against your chest, your legs on either side of me. In the steaming water

Curled up in bed with the universe against our window.

I still remember the little things

The kitchen pantries. The sofa bed.

Chocolates on the table and balloons overhead.

On the beach we picked up shells and named them and wrote our names in the sand

building castles in the water

And in the night we danced until dawn

My feet barefoot against the rug when not in heels

Drinking tequila sunrise and beers, laughing in the smoke

Turning 25 to the lights and the dancers

Buying souvenirs, long shot glasses with our names engraved on the side

and a heart box made of tiny cracked shells

as small and quaint as your heartbeat

to keep the shells we found on the sand

And one tiny miracle of a silver chain

with a half heart and a key that read

He who holds the key can open my heart

much like the heart keyhole on your

front door

Casinos late at night and breakfast at four a.m.

Before we snuggled up again to the bay view

one last glass of champagne before we left

the universe that morning

TAKE ME

I.

Take me to the Underworld,

Lead me to Hades, who will crown me dancer of the eternal night,

Keeper of the souls, huntress of death, apprentice to Hermes.

Take me to Lethe where I may forget you,

Styx, where I may make my oath to abandon you

Cocytus will be well suited for when I lament you

Acheron for when I cry for you

Phlegethon for when I wish to burn your photographs, collect

their ashes, make them dust, have them guarded by Cerberus himself.

I will take over for Persephone, I will even pay your fare,

place the coin on your sweet lips, as sweet and sickly as the sorrow of Demeter,

so that dutiful Charon may take you there.

II.

And when and if you are gone, I will breathe new life unto myself,

breathe as Athena breathed life into man's clay shape,

and burn myself like the Phoenix, rise above your ashes, greater

than any torch of fire brought back from the sun, more divine than Venus,

as wise as Athena, as chaste as Artemis, shooting, transcending these barriers

with my silver arrows.

And if there is a chance you will not be gone, I won't grieve for the sorrows of mankind

But look in the bottom of Pandora's box, the very bottom, where Hope once lay.

I will be the face that launched a thousand ships,

The face you will never forget, the face you will fight for.

I will carry the world for Atlas for your return, if only a bit,

and perform my Twelve Labors without pause,

and wherever slaughtered I will spring a new head.

My gifts for you will be as multitudinous as the Hydra,

my secrets as mysterious and unconquerable as the Sphinx's smile,

my charm as alluring as the lone Siren who calls out in the song that never fails,

my devotion as faithful as Calypso's cruel clutch,

And you, my Odysseus, will sail on, a wiser man.

III.

Come back to me, your Penelope, whether ten years or twenty,

Make your feet hit the soils of Ithaca, let your wrath be unleashed on my gluttonous suitors,

Meet again with Telemachus, make my home a happy one once more, raise me like Helen,

elevate me again, make me fly like Icarus

devour me like the sun but do not burn my wings,

Let me live with you in the Elysian Fields,

Let our love make Apollo sing.

SHAHIDA ARABI

ONE LIVING BEING

"*Constantly regard the universe as one living being, having one substance and one soul; and observe how all things have reference to one perception, the perception of this one living being; and how all things act with one movement; and how all things are the cooperating causes of all things which exist; observe too the continuous spinning of the thread and the contexture of the web.*"

—Marcus Aurelius, *Meditations*

The thread has gone loose.

The web is a flimsy garment on a half-naked lady

whose lies are like gossamer,

so weak that once they're pulled they fall

though they still have the power to entrap and ensnare and devour.

Those two people who once co-created, spun avidly

are now dancing in the Elysian Field that is the past.

I wish I could visit them. Now I am sitting like Tantalus with an empty cup of nothing.

The thirst has faded but there is an old ache that reminds me I once used to drink from this cup.

CATECHISM.

The room was once silent like church during prayer

Filled with the noises of wet kisses, hands rubbing backs, discreet laughter under the covers

An arm flung over my body, hand dancing with hand, fingers grazing the tips of fingers

Tongues wrestling to speak, speechless

But then

Eyes wide open I find you shut

Your back to me facing the other way

Arms no longer seek arms, hands have forgotten their promised land

Morning shafts of sunlight break through

I try to talk myself into listening.

No questions need be asked.

Like church bells the recognition dangles, clangs, pounds in my ears

Waiting for me to hear them.

Not anymore.

Whispered excuses and a gentle halfhearted pat on the back later

I lay on the bed alone with my hands spiderlike.

now mouths gape open, cheap talk floods through the walls

Watching the ceiling, hearing the laughter from the next room

I am curled up waiting for the flimsy web

to break like thin gossamer

so I can wrap the bits around me like film

and relive the sordid tale

FIRST TIME IN ECUADOR

You called the girls you liked preciosa

and me linda

beautiful

smart

quirky

small

when we lie in bed

I curl around your waist

like a cat purring at your feet

As I relish the feeling of my head

buried in your chest

sleeping at the nook of your neck

Remembering

the way your lips grazed my head

when you first met me

and I danced so fast I twirled a dozen times

just holding your hand.

even though we have

shut some doors

you still find the gateway through the gaps

and in the chasms

somehow we poke our fingers

through and they

wrap around each other

and

clench.

FAIRY GODMOTHER

Her skin, a trail of red marks,

a love letter written to herself in the language of hate.

I ask her what she needed and what she has gotten.

A lullaby, a prayer, a kind reminder, was what she needed.

And all she received was his cold, callous pleasure at her pain.

His razor-sharp words had cut her deep—

Is it so astonishing that someone after a nightmare of life might just want to sleep?

Her wish was my command, but all she wanted was a glass tomb to rest in.

Is it no wonder that when God laughed,

She sliced herself in halves? Like a magic trick

You pulled out your cards, asked her to choose

But your greatest trick was disappearing

And hers was to make herself anew—

This is the secret—

She cuts and she cuts so she can sew again.

GURU

Nothing more calming

than a false mask, a veneer,

the guru-like status of a nobody

marked with the stamp of condescension.

Beware the yogi who does not know the meaning of compassion off the mat.

The meditator who will silence

the sound of others breathing through their pain

and speaking quietly to the voice inside of them

rather than echo loudly and blindly the voice of their leader.

Just to see them squirm.

Beware the healer who builds for you a trapdoor

And calls it the only portal to the truth.

MARTYR

The sky rips open with just one tear in its fabric

Dead hopes scratch at the skin and the heart plummets

the pain of imperfection and the solid grip of choice

you can choose to leave at any time

but you don't.

Walking on water leaves you dehydrated

so you scoop up a palmful of it

hoping not to drown and open your mouth

and drink.

Water turns to blood and blood into flesh into water again

the mind becomes nothing less than matter observing matter

in the spinning of one thought, one becomes another

the sky becomes as clear as the dark pupil

the pulpit shrinks and you are left with one speaker

you drag your feet and take rest on the ground

loving the solid feeling of a different miracle

until morning, when you choose to tread the water again;

because all communion has a price.

SHAHIDA ARABI

DUST

He turns his words into food and she starves until
She's seen God again.
Prayer softens the shell until she's suffocating
the cocoon of forethought strangles her
in the straitjacket of his confession booth
she knows he will begin again
but for now he seeks repentance,
with blood on his hands and amen.

INFINITY

In the afternoon we see the paintings of galaxies

In the evening we step into a room filled with mirrors,
LED lights and water

All reflecting us back into space and possibilities

Each reflection is a tiny galaxy

Waiting to show us a new world.

In the air the city stretches like gold for miles

Empty canyons and fields of desert

Extend to buildings and skyscrapers

Nothingness and lights all in one stretch of the eye.

ABOUT THE AUTHOR

Shahida Arabi is a graduate of Columbia University graduate school and the bestselling author of *The Smart Girl's Guide to Self-Care* and *Becoming the Narcissist's Nightmare*, a #1 Amazon bestseller. Her work has been featured on The Huffington Post, The National Domestic Violence Hotline, MOGUL and Thought Catalog. Her blog, Self-Care Haven, has reached millions of survivors all over the world and her articles have been endorsed by numerous bestselling authors, mental health professionals and award-winning bloggers.

Twitter: twitter.com/selfcarehaven

Facebook: facebook.com/selfcarehaven

Website: selfcarehaven.wordpress.com

ABOUT THE PUBLISHER

Thought Catalog Books is a publishing house owned by The Thought & Expression Company, an independent media group based in Brooklyn, NY. Founded in 2010, we are committed to facilitating thought and expression. We exist to help people become better communicators and listeners in order to engender a more exciting, attentive, and imaginative world.

www.thought.is

www.thoughtcatalog.com

Explore Great Books

www.thoughtcatalog.com/books